The Psalms of King David
© Demi 2024

Wisdom Tales in an imprint of World Wisdom, Inc.

Library of Congress Cataloging-in-Publication Data

Names: Demi, author, illustrator.
Title: The Psalms of King David / Demi.
Description: Bloomington, Indiana : Wisdom Tales, [2024] | Audience: Grades 2-3 | Summary: "The Bible tells us that King David was a man after God's own heart (1 Samuel 13:14), chosen by Him to lead his people Israel. David began life as a simple shepherd, but his fearless courage and unshakable faith in God would see him slay the Philistine giant Goliath and become a celebrated warrior. After the death of King Saul, the Lord God would establish David as king over Israel. Soon, he would go on to conquer the fortress city of Jerusalem and install the Ark of the Covenant within its walls. But, above all, King David would be remembered as the inspired poet and harpist who composed the Biblical Psalms to the Lord his God. Award-winning author, Demi, recounts the dramatic story of David, the shepherd who rose to become king"-- Provided by publisher.
Identifiers: LCCN 2023014321 (print) | LCCN 2023014322 (ebook) | ISBN 9781957670027 (hardback) | ISBN 9781957670034 (epub)
Subjects: LCSH: David, King of Israel--Juvenile literature. | Bible. Psalms--Juvenile literature. | Bible. Old Testament--Biography--Juvenile literature. | Jews--Kings and rulers--Biography--Juvenile literature.
Classification: LCC BS580.D3 D5155 2024 (print) | LCC BS580.D3 (ebook) | DDC 223/.2--dc23/eng/20230616
LC record available at https://lccn.loc.gov/2023014321
LC ebook record available at https://lccn.loc.gov/2023014322

Printed in China on acid-free paper

For information address Wisdom Tales,
P.O. Box 2682, Bloomington, Indiana, 47402-2682
www.wisdomtalespress.com

THE PSALMS OF KING DAVID

DEMI

✦ Wisdom Tales ✦

A little time before 1000 BCE, a boy named David was born in Bethlehem, to Jesse and Nitzevet of the tribe of Judah. He was their eighth son.

Every day David herded their sheep and every day he sang songs to God on his little harp.

Samuel, the great judge and prophet of Israel, was looking throughout the land to find and anoint their next king. For Saul, the present king, had disobeyed the laws and commandments of the Lord God.

When Samuel came to Bethlehem and saw Jesse's seven strong and handsome sons, he thought one of them must surely be the next king.

But the Lord God said to Samuel, "The Lord does not see as man sees; for man looks at the outward appearance, but the Lord looks at the heart."

Samuel then asked Jesse, "Are all the young men here?"

And Jesse answered, "There remains yet the youngest, and there he is, keeping the sheep."

When Samuel saw David, the Lord God said: "Arise, anoint him; for this is the one!" (1 Samuel 16:7-13). And so Samuel anointed David as the next king of Israel.

When David returned to his flocks he sang with the spirit of the Lord: "The heavens declare the glory of God; the skies proclaim the work of His hands" (Psalm 19:1).

And again: "The pastures are clothed with flocks; the valleys also are covered with grain; they shout for joy, they also sing. . . . All the earth shall worship You and sing praises to You" (Psalm 65:12-13; 66:4).

One day a powerful lion grabbed a little lamb from David's flock. David felt afraid and wounded in his own heart and soul, but he said to himself, "It is God that gives me power too!" And suddenly, feeling that power, David chased after the lion. With his slingshot he aimed right at the lion's head and instantly killed it. With God's power, David had saved the little lamb.

Then David sang:

"The Lord is my shepherd;

I shall not want.

He makes me to lie down in green pastures;

He leads me beside the still waters.

He restores my soul;

He leads me in the paths of righteousness

For His name's sake.

Yea, though I walk through the valley of the shadow of death,

I will fear no evil;

For You are with me;

Your rod and Your staff, they comfort me.

You prepare a table before me in the presence of my enemies;

You anoint my head with oil;

My cup runs over.

Surely goodness and mercy shall follow me

All the days of my life;

And I will dwell in the house of the Lord forever" (Psalm 23).

Not only had King Saul disobeyed
the laws of the Lord God,
but he was also going mad.
His servants said the king needed music to soothe
his soul, and they called for David,
who they heard could play the harp.

When David played his beautiful music,
all the king's demons disappeared.
For David sang of his love and trust in God
and the joy in His creation.
Then King Saul loved David
and made him his armor-bearer.

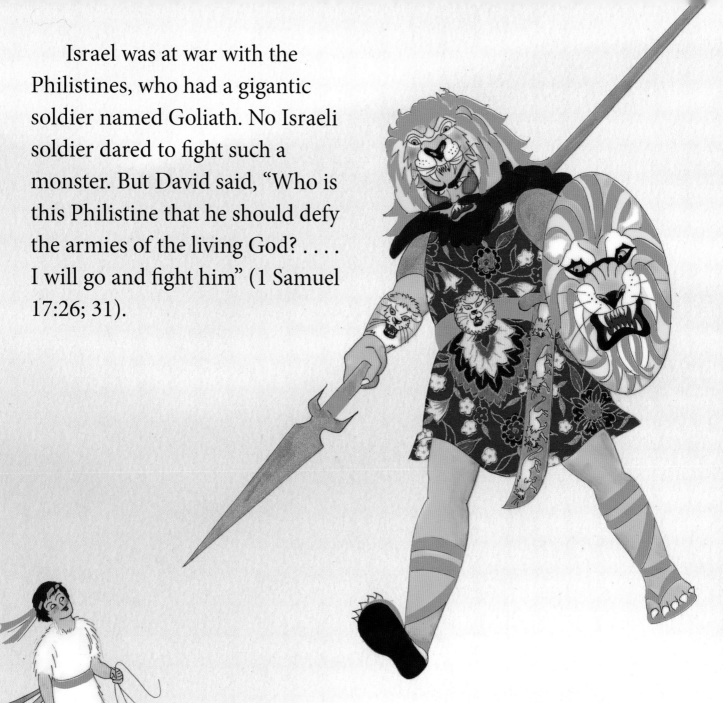

Israel was at war with the Philistines, who had a gigantic soldier named Goliath. No Israeli soldier dared to fight such a monster. But David said, "Who is this Philistine that he should defy the armies of the living God? . . . . I will go and fight him" (1 Samuel 17:26; 31).

"You are not able to go against this Philistine," said King Saul, "for you are a youth, and he a man of war!"

David replied, "The Lord, who delivered me from the paw of the lion, He will deliver me from the hand of this Philistine" (1 Samuel 17:33; 37).

David refused armor. Instead he carried his slingshot and picked up five stones from a brook. Goliath mocked David, saying: "Come to me, and I will give your flesh to the birds of the air and the beasts of the field!"

David answered, "You come to me with a sword, with a spear, and a javelin. But I come to you in the name of the Lord . . . who this day will deliver you into my hand" (1 Samuel 17:44-45). Putting a stone in his slingshot, he aimed at the center of Goliath's forehead and let it fly. Piercing Goliath's skull, the giant fell to earth and was instantly killed.

The Philistine army fled, and David was the hero of all Israel and Judah. In the cities, people sang and danced and shouted, "Saul has slain his thousands, and David his ten thousands!" (1 Samuel 18:7).

David sang:

"The Lord is my light and my salvation;
Whom shall I fear?
The Lord is the strength of my life;
Of whom shall I be afraid?
When the wicked came against me
To eat up my flesh,
My enemies and foes,
They stumbled and fell.
Though an army may encamp against me,
My heart shall not fear;
Though war may rise against me,
In this I will be confident" (Psalm 27:1-3).

But now King Saul was maddened with jealousy of David. He twice tried to kill him by hurling his javelin while David was playing the harp. Twice David escaped.

Then King Saul and his army chased David, who escaped and hid in the cave of Adullam, then in the wilderness of Ziph, and last in the wilderness crags of En Gedi with wild goats.

At first David sang: "My God, my God, why have you forsaken me? (Psalm 22:1). But gathering strength, he sang: "But You, O Lord, are a shield for me, my glory and the One who lifts up my head. I cried to the Lord with my voice, and He heard me from His holy hill. . . . Arise, O Lord; save me, O my God!" (Psalm 3:3-7).

Multitudes followed and
joined David in the wilderness,
for they all loved him greatly.

One day King Saul came to rest in a wilderness cave
where David was hiding. David could have killed him
on the spot. But he chose not to because he knew it was
forbidden to kill the Lord God's appointed king.
And so David only cut off a piece of the king's robe
to shame him.

Another time, while King Saul slept,
David crept into his camp and stole his
water jug and spear. When King Saul
saw that he had been shamed again,
he wept and said to David:
   "You are more righteous than I;
for you have rewarded me with good,
whereas I have rewarded you with evil"
(1 Samuel 24:17). Shortly thereafter he died.

Now David was king of Judah. Soon after, David was anointed king of all Israel. Next he prepared to march on Jerusalem and make it his holy capital. The rocky mountain fortress was held so strongly by the Jebusites that they mocked King David by saying, "The blind and the deaf are enough to defend these walls!" (2 Samuel 5:8).

But King David knew that below the fortress there was a hidden spring, and a tunnel that was cut straight up through the rock to draw up the water. King David and his men went secretly to the hidden spring and climbed up the tunnel in the rock. Quickly they surprised the Jebusites and took the city.

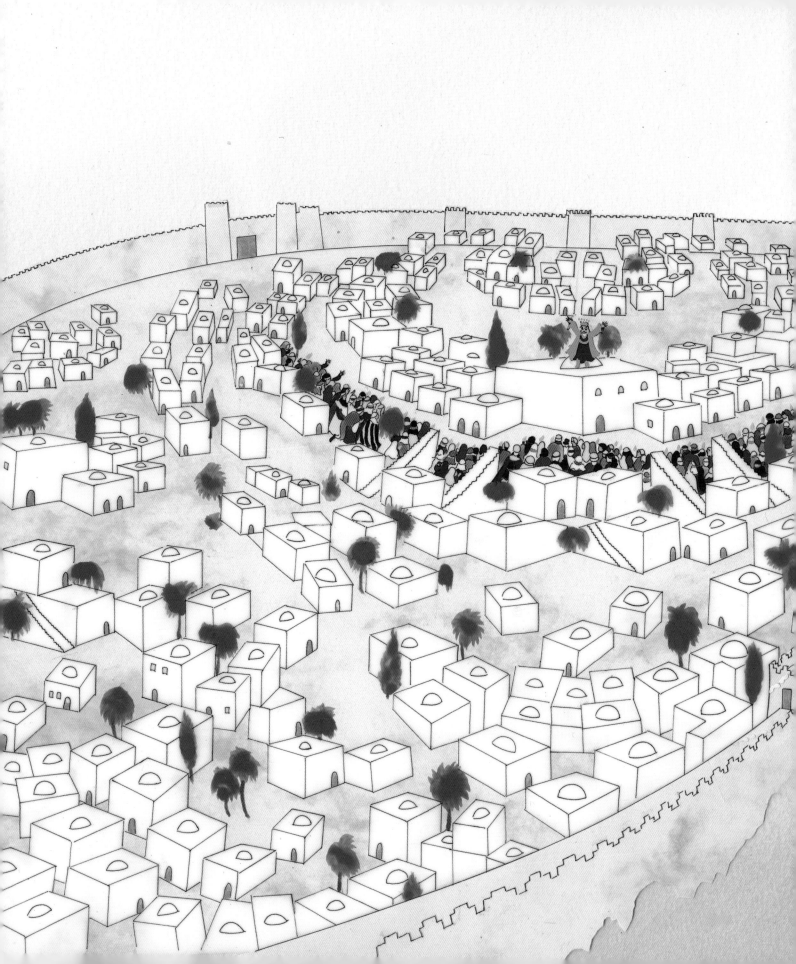

Rejoicing and celebrating, all the followers of King David then moved into Jerusalem. They beautified the city and made it the capital of Israel, and called it the City of David.

King David sang: "Great is the Lord, and greatly to be praised in the city of our God, in His holy mountain. Beautiful in elevation, the joy of the whole earth, is Mount Zion" (Psalm 48:1-2).

King David also sang: "Our feet have been standing within your gates, O Jerusalem! . . . . Pray for the peace of Jerusalem: May they prosper who love you. Peace be within your walls, prosperity within your palaces" (Psalm 122:2; 6-7).

Then King David and all of Israel brought the Ark of the Covenant of God into Jerusalem with shouting, dancing, and singing.

Everyone made offerings to God, and King David sang, "I will lift up my eyes to the hills: from whence comes my help? My help comes from the Lord, who made heaven and earth. . . . The Lord shall preserve you from all evil; He shall preserve your soul. The Lord shall preserve your going out and your coming in from this time forth, and even forevermore" (Psalm 121:1-2; 7-8).

King David, the sweet psalmist of Israel, sang many more psalms unto the Lord God. As one of the greatest kings that ever lived, he conquered an empire that stretched from Egypt to the far Euphrates. After ruling Israel for forty years, King David died at the age of seventy.